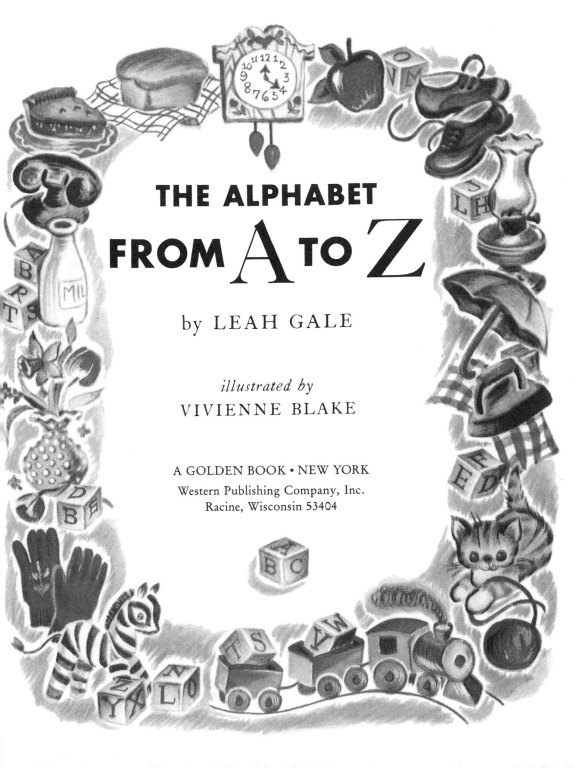

THE ALPHABET
FROM A TO Z

by LEAH GALE

illustrated by
VIVIENNE BLAKE

A GOLDEN BOOK • NEW YORK
Western Publishing Company, Inc.
Racine, Wisconsin 53404

THE LITTLE GOLDEN BOOKS
ARE PREPARED UNDER THE SUPERVISION OF
MARY REED, Ph.D.
ASSISTANT PROFESSOR OF EDUCATION
TEACHERS COLLEGE, COLUMBIA UNIVERSITY

A COMMEMORATIVE FACSIMILE EDITION PUBLISHED ON THE OCCASION OF
THE 50TH ANNIVERSARY OF LITTLE GOLDEN BOOKS

Jimmy in his house can see
The alphabet from A to Z.

A is the Apple for Jimmy to bite;

B is the Bed

that he sleeps in at night;

C is the Clock
that goes,
"Tick, tock, tick;"

D is the Dish for the doggie to lick.

E is the Engine
with eight shiny wheels;

F is the Fork
Jimmy uses at meals;

G

G is his Gloves,
the red woolen pair;

H

H is the Hat
for Jimmy to wear.

I is the Iron
for pressing his clothes;

J is the Jacket

he wears when it snows;

K is the Kitten

he found in the park;

L is the Lamp
that he lights after dark.

M is the Milk
that always tastes good;

N is the Nail that
he hammers in wood;

O is the Oven where
Mother bakes bread;

P

P is the Pie
with the cherries so red.

Q is the Quilt
that's too warm for July;

R is the Rubbers
to keep his feet dry;

S is the Shoe

Jimmy ties with a string;

T is the Telephone,
ding-a-ling, ling.

U

U is the Umbrella
to use when it showers;

V is the Vase
in which Jimmy puts flowers;

W is the Window
that's sunny all day;

X is the Xylophone
for Jimmy to play.

Y is the Yarn
Mother uses to mend;

Z is the Zebra

Jimmy got from a friend.

Here are thirteen letters,
Each begins a word.

Match them with these pictures—
Things you've seen and heard.

A	a	*a*	APPLE
B	b	*b*	BED
C	c	*c*	CLOCK
D	d	*d*	DISH
E	e	*e*	ENGINE
F	f	*f*	FORK
G	g	*g*	GLOVES
H	h	*h*	HAT
I	i	*i*	IRON
J	j	*j*	JACKET
K	k	*k*	KITTEN
L	l	*l*	LAMP
M	m	*m*	MILK

Thirteen other letters
Complete the alphabet;

Jimmy knew the pictures—
How many can you get?

N	n	*n*	NAIL
O	o	*o*	OVEN
P	p	*p*	PIE
Q	q	*q*	QUILT
R	r	*r*	RUBBERS
S	s	*s*	SHOES
T	t	*t*	TELEPHONE
U	u	*u*	UMBRELLA
V	v	*v*	VASE
W	w	*w*	WINDOW
X	x	*x*	XYLOPHONE
Y	y	*y*	YARN
Z	z	*z*	ZEBRA